The
Gift
of

SPIRITUAL

ABUNDANCE

THE GIFT OF
SPIRITUAL ABUNDACE

Five Principles for Being Happy and Fulfilled Right Now

by JEFF CARREIRA

The Gift of

Spiritual Abundance

By Jeff Carreira

Copyright © 2020

Emergence Education & Jeff Carreira

All rights reserved. Except as permitted under U.S. Copyright Act of 1976, no part of this publication may be reproduced, distributed, or transmitted in any form or by any means, or stored in a database or retrieval system, without the prior written permission of the publisher.

ISBN-13: 978-0-9995658-9-6

Emergence Education Press
P.O. Box 63767, Philadelphia, PA 19147
www.EmergenceEducation.com

Cover and interior design by Silvia Rodrigues

iii

Contents

Introduction IX

Part 1: What Is Spiritual Abundance? 1

   The Inherent Fullness of Life. 3

   Spiritual Abundance Is More than a Winning Attitude . . 11

   Giving Your Gift to the World 19

   Trust in Life 27

   Abundance Is a New Operating System 35

Part 2: The Five Principles of Spiritual Abundance. . . 43

   Know What You're Passionate About 45

   Only Abundance Creates Abundance 53

   Abundance Only Happens Now 61

   The Life You are Living is Already The
Life of Your Dreams. 69

   Do What You Love Because You Love It. 77

About the Author. 84

*"The greatest discovery
of any generation is that you can alter
your life by altering your attitude."*

— WILLIAM JAMES

VIII

Introduction

This is a short book, less than 5000 words in fact, and I kept it short on purpose.

Mark Twain once famously said, "I didn't have time to write a short letter, so I wrote a long one instead."

Well in this case, I decided it was worth taking the time to write a short book, and I've been working on it for nearly two years.

Why all the effort? Because the principles I want to share are so unimaginably simple and, at the same time, so subtle and profound that it is the easiest thing in the world to miss them completely by burying them under unnecessary detail and explanation.

The challenge in communicating these principles is how simple, immediate and easy they actually are.

In this book, you will discover how to be happy and fulfilled, but the solution is so immediately available that you won't believe it.

My fear in writing this book has been that no one will believe it. They will think, "Sure maybe that worked for him, but it won't work for me." I'm afraid that you won't give these principles a chance by applying them for a long enough time in your own life to find out that they actually work.

So, I decided to write the shortest book I could, using clear and simple language.

Please don't look for deeper esoteric meaning behind these words. They mean exactly what they say.

The challenge of this book is accepting that the principles in it are as simple and immediate as they are.

PART I

What Is Spiritual Abundance?

THE INHERENT
FULLNESS OF LIFE

Spiritual abundance is an inner attitude born out of the recognition that nothing is missing and that you already have everything you really need to be fulfilled.

Cultivating spiritual abundance means building a habitual tendency to notice the bounty and goodness that is always already here.

This inner tendency opens our eyes to the boundless blessing of being alive.

It isn't a denial of all that is challenging, painful and unjust. It is an acceptance of the fact that challenge, pain and injustice can't be entirely avoided. And, even more importantly, it is the recognition that, on the whole, in spite of life's unpleasant and even traumatic aspects, it is still a blessing to be alive in a beautiful world riding the roller coaster of being human.

We all experience spiritual abundance from time to time. For instance, when we see a perfect sunset over the ocean and stand transfixed by the sheer magnitude of the beauty of this Earth; or when we hold a newborn baby in our arms and can hardly contain the joy that rushes through our heart; or when we meet an old friend for the first time in years and burst into tears because everything we ever felt for them is still there.

These wondrous moments leave us feeling happy and full, even if only temporarily, because they reflect back to us the true beauty, mystery and magnitude of life.

After an event like this, we find ourselves open, available, generous and grateful.

The aim of this book is to show you that this depth of gratitude and openness of heart can become your ongoing experience of being alive.

I have devoted my life to the discovery and realization of spiritual awakening, and I've come to the conclusion that spiritual abundance is the natural expression of spiritual awakening. They are flip sides of the same coin and cultivating one inevitably leads to the other. In this book you will find out how.

> *Cultivating spiritual abundance means building a habitual tendency to notice the bounty and goodness that is always already here.*

SPIRITUAL ABUNDANCE IS MORE
THAN A WINNING ATTITUDE

One thing that I want to be clear about from the start is that spiritual abundance is not the same thing as having a winning attitude.

When I was a young boy, I would sometimes stay up late at night and turn on my black and white TV to watch the only thing that was on: infomercials. One of these featured a professional football quarterback and a self-help coach who is now famous. I was entranced every single time I saw it.

They were boldly declaring that you could create exactly the life you wanted if you adopted a winning attitude. The two secrets of a winning attitude were: single-pointed focus on achieving success and retraining your perception to see opportunities rather than obstacles.

They explained how so many of us are burdened by a habit of always seeing the obstacles that block us from what we want. We no sooner begin on the path toward our dreams when we are confronted by all of the obstacles that stand in our way. Too often, we simply stop there and never move any closer to the life we truly want. Even at a young age, I was hooked by the creative power that these two men were inviting me to embrace.

To be honest, I still think this kind of winning attitude message is awesome and important for all of us to adopt. In fact, a few years ago, I had the chance to attend a daylong seminar with the same self-help coach that I watched in my youth. He was more amazing in person than I remember. Even more impressive was the energy amongst the thousands of people who attended the event. Many people told me about how their lives had been transformed by adopting a winning attitude.

A winning attitude is amazing, but what I am presenting as spiritual abundance is something different. Even with a winning attitude, we too often find ourselves driven to achieve more than what we have. A winning attitude can give us the energy to succeed, but it doesn't necessarily change the game we're in.

The first thing you need to understand is that spiritual abundance does not originate from a sense of needing to create the life of your dreams. It starts from the recognition that the life you're living is already the life of your dreams, as long as you look at it with new eyes. The perspective that you will explore in this book isn't about winning, it's about recognizing that you've already won.

> *...spiritual abundance does not originate from a sense of needing to create the life of your dreams. It starts from the recognition that the life you're living is already the life of your dreams...*

GIVING YOUR GIFT
TO THE WORLD

To cultivate spiritual abundance, all you need to do is learn to recognize the abundance you already have and feel grateful for it. When you're happy and grateful for the things you already have, you feel abundance in your life, and the feeling of abundance attracts more abundance. By establishing a practice of abundance, you can generate a positive upward momentum that will carry you to ever-increasing levels of fulfillment.

We are all conditioned by a powerful cultural habit of looking for what's wrong and what's missing. Cultivating spiritual abundance means retraining yourself to see what's here and what's working. As our orientation shifts from an assumption of lack to an assumption of abundance, we naturally begin to experience a sense of existential gratitude. Over time, we'll find that this new orientation allows us to be open, receptive and generous in relationship to life because we are no longer preoccupied by what we don't have, and we are increasingly aware of how much we do have. This attitude of abundance is contagious. As we become more generous, we find that life is more generous with us.

Cultivating spiritual abundance naturally leads to expressions of generosity and open heartedness. When you feel full and plentiful, you have no need for self-protection. You are naturally open, available, vulnerable and generous of spirit.

It is in our nature as humans to want to give. The nature of life is generous and full, and in our heart of hearts, we want to be an expression of that same abundant generosity.

Life is about giving, and in many ways, we've been taught exactly the opposite. Too often we're trained to think that life is about what we can get out of it, but the purpose of life is not to accumulate things for yourself. The reason we are here is to spend ourselves completely. And I don't mean exhaust yourself in the rat race until you can't get out of bed. I mean giving everything you have of value so that you can leave this life feeling completely satisfied, knowing that you held nothing back.

The greatest realization is knowing that you took all the love in your heart, all the joy, all the blessings you've been given, and gave them back to the world. If you do that, then, when it's time to leave this life behind, you'll go freely without regrets and with no reason to return.

We're all different. We all have different gifts and it is a thrill to discover what our unique gift to give actually is. Everybody's gift is different, everybody's qualities are different, and everyone has their own unique contribution to make to the world. Yours might be completely different than someone else's, but that's irrelevant. What matters is that it's yours to give, and the ultimate satisfaction in life is found by giving it.

The nature of life is generous and full, and in our heart of hearts, we want to be an expression of that same abundant generosity.

TRUST IN LIFE

To live a life of spiritual abundance you need a profound degree of trust in life. Most of us don't start out with this depth of trust in life. Life's inevitable challenges and traumas leave us mistrustful and defended. The unconscious habit of mistrust hides the bounty of life behind a protective wall of fear, worry and self-concern. We are left feeling compelled to remain on guard against harm. If we want to live a life of spiritual abundance, we have to find a way to recover our ability to trust.

In my spiritual work, I use the practice of meditation as a tool for recovering existential trust. The instructions for meditation that I give are simply to sit still with your eyes closed and not make a problem out of anything that arises. I call it The Art of Conscious Contentment. And don't let the simplicity of it fool you. Following these instructions for meditation is an invitation to a profound journey of awakening.

When we sit with the intention to not make a problem out of anything that arises, we quickly discover how subtle and challenging it is to not have a problem. Our habits of finding fault and of constantly manipulating our experience to get something out of it are so pervasive that they seem impossible to avoid. But, if you stick with it, you will begin to relax all of your reactive habits of self-defensive control. You will gradually learn to sit and just be with whatever arises. You will find it more and more delightful to settle into this profound state of restful surrender.

If you keep at it, you will make a life-altering discovery. You will discover that nothing is actually wrong with life. Yes, of course, there are aspects of life that are painful, but they are not wrong; they are the natural and inevitable consequence of circumstance. In spite of the fact that there are many aspects of life that we want to be different, there is nothing inherently wrong with any of it.

When you see this deeply for yourself, something profound shifts inside you. You recognize how much of your energy has been consumed by the fight against all the things you have perceived as wrong, and now that you don't have to fight that fight anymore, you suddenly have so much more energy and attention for living.

There may be a part of you that has a hard time with the idea that there's nothing wrong with life. It's important to realize that we are not talking about a blind and naive acceptance of the way things are. This is not about being resigned to pain and suffering, and it's not about pretending there's nothing wrong. It's about seeing that there is something very positive going on that is bigger than any particular circumstance that might be painful or unjust. We see that life as a whole is a good thing even though bad things happen.

There is a direct relationship between spiritual abundance and spiritual awakening.

Spiritual awakening can be defined as the discovery of the inherent goodness of life, and a life of spiritual abundance is the natural outcome of this discovery.

> *There is a direct relationship between spiritual abundance and spiritual awakening.*

ABUNDANCE IS A NEW
OPERATING SYSTEM

Some people, when hearing all this, will start to feel that if they let go and trust this much, they will lose their drive. They believe that the sense that something is wrong is the source of energy that spurs them to act. They fear that if they realize that there is nothing wrong, they might not be motivated to do anything at all.

It makes sense to wonder about this because we've all been conditioned to respond to lack, and we've become unconsciously convinced that lack is the only operating system in the universe. What motivates us, we assume, are all the things that we want and need. We see dissatisfaction as an energy source and we believe that, if we're satisfied, we won't feel any urgency to do anything. We need to have problems to keep us going.

We have been enculturated into an operating system driven by lack and scarcity. Lack is a powerful driver, but it only takes you so far, and there is a more powerful operating system that can move us. It's an operating system that runs on possibility. That operating system is not driven by what's missing or what's broken; it's driven by what's possible. If you step into the operating system of possibility, your heart begins to swell because you see more and more of what's possible for you and for everyone else.

Living from the operating system of abundance will make a huge difference in your life. Let's think about it for just a minute. Imagine two people. The first person has a personality that leaves them constantly seeing everything that's wrong. They immediately become aware of what's wrong in every situation and they are generally frustrated with life because they don't feel like they're ever going to have what they need. Can you imagine such a person? It's probably us on some days.

The second person has a different personality. They're the kind of person who tends to see what's working and what's available to them in every situation. They don't tend to see what's missing; they tend to see what's possible. Can you imagine that person? It's probably us on our better days.

Now imagine that both of these people live for the next ten years; one tending to see what's wrong, the other tending to see what's possible. Of course, this is an oversimplification, but just to make the point: After ten years, whose life do you think you'd prefer to be living? Most people I've come across say the second person and that's because we already know, from our own experience, that an attitude of spiritual abundance inevitably leads to a better life.

...an attitude of spiritual abundance inevitably leads to a better life.

PART 2

The Five Principles of Spiritual Abundance

KNOW WHAT YOU'RE PASSIONATE ABOUT

Now that we've explored what spiritual abundance is, it's time to explore the principles that allow us to live it.

From one point of view, the ultimate principle of spiritual abundance is well known. It's just not lived very often.

If you want to live a life of spiritual abundance, you need to live your passion.

How many people haven't heard that already, right?

But wait, it's not that simple. Even though we've all heard it before, we might not have thought about it deeply enough to know what it really means. All of the principles we're about to discuss boil down to this one: Live your passion.

But before you can live your passion, you have to know what you are passionate about. This may sound too obvious to be significant, but don't tune out yet, there's more to it than you might think.

You see, we often have a lot of ideas about what our passions are, and often they don't turn out to be what we're authentically passionate about at all.

The first principle of spiritual abundance is discovering what you're truly passionate about. You probably already know what it is. It is probably something that you already love to spend time doing but have marginalized to some small corner of your life.

Whatever that is, whatever you love to do the most, you need to consider what your life would look like if that was the main thing you were involved with every day.

I realize that you might object and say this couldn't be the main focus of your life because you could never make a living like that.

My experience tells me that if you want to live a life of spiritual abundance, you'll have to take the risk of putting the thing that you love the most at the very center of your life.

Whatever you love to do the most, you need to consider what your life would look like if that was the main thing you were involved with every day.

ONLY ABUNDANCE
CREATES ABUNDANCE

The second principle of spiritual abundance is more subtle and profound than the first. It is simply the fact that the only thing that can generate abundance is abundance.

The principle recipe for abundance is that abundance leads to more abundance and nothing else does.

We often mistakenly think that we can use something else to generate abundance. We try using effort or willpower to get abundance but, in the end, you always get more of what you're giving. So, if you're making effort to be abundant, you don't get abundance, you get the opportunity to make more effort.

Thinking in terms of doing something now to get something later is the essence of lack because it's rooted in the idea that something is missing now that you imagine you'll get later.

Anything you do now to become abundant later reinforces the experience of lacking now. There is nothing you can do now to become abundant later that won't reinforce the exact experience of lack you're trying to get away from.

To be abundant, you must find a way to be abundant in your life exactly the way it is now.

If you can't live abundance in the life you're living right now, you won't be able to find abundance anywhere. There is nothing that can make your life abundant.

Abundance isn't about wealth or accumulation. Abundance isn't about having anything. It is a shift in our relationship to being alive in the first place.

I've worked with people who earn a great deal of money and have a lot of things but are still living with a debilitating sense of lack and scarcity. They're living in lack with a lot of money. You can live in lack with a lot of money just as easily as you can live in lack with none.

You can live in lack in any lifestyle you want. Lack is not something that happens to you because of circumstance. It's a habitual way of relating to life as a whole.

As we've already discussed, to live abundance you have to break the habit of being in lack and develop a habit of living in abundance.

If you do this, nothing in your life will need to change because you'll be living in abundance already. Everything will already be fine and, as a result, everything will change, because an abundant spirit is incredibly attractive - not just to people but to everything. Abundance leads to more abundance. That's the way it works.

To be abundant, you must find a way to be abundant in your life exactly the way it is now.

ABUNDANCE ONLY HAPPENS NOW

The third principle of spiritual abundance is that it can only be lived right now, in the life you're already in the middle of. If you're living abundance now, you will inevitably attract more abundance because you always get more of what you already have.

If you're living in lack trying to become abundant, you're going to end up living in more lack, trying even harder to become abundant.

I've seen people spend decades of their lives constantly thinking they're going to get out of lack by doing the next thing, only to find that the next thing doesn't change the picture at all. They keep going year after year. And just like any habit, if you develop a momentum of lack, it becomes harder and harder to break it no matter how much you achieve or accumulate.

The best thing you can do, if you want to live abundance, is stop trying to live abundance and start living abundance right now, exactly the way things are.

Find a way to shift into a sense of dramatic abundance and appreciation for the life you are already living.

Of course, it's easy to say, "All we need to do is be abundant now." But there's always a big part of us that consciously and unconsciously is going to complain, "You just can't BE abundant. That just doesn't make sense. How is that ever going to work? You're just pretending to be abundant. You can't just turn abundance on. Something needs to change first."

This kind of thinking keeps us stuck in a life in which we never feel like we've made it. There is always one more thing that needs to change before we can be happy with the life we're living.

Can you move past the belief that abundance isn't possible for you right now?

If you think abundance is only possible later, even if you really believe in the possibility of abundance and are sure you will have it after just one more change, abundance will remain out of reach.

That's because believing that abundance will come later simultaneously means believing that abundance isn't possible now. And that will never change. There will always be a later. There will always be something else to do. There will always be another tweak to make in your life.

If you're living abundance now, you will inevitably attract more abundance because you always get more of what you already have.

THE LIFE YOU ARE LIVING IS
ALREADY THE LIFE OF YOUR DREAMS

The fourth principle of spiritual abundance asks us to focus on the aspects of our life that are already full, because our life always feels full if that is where we put our attention.

Someone recently gave me one of the greatest compliments I ever received. She started by sharing a powerful way of understanding abundance.

To her, living an abundant life should result in being able to do what you want, when you want, with who you want, for the reasons you want. Then, she told me that I was the only person she'd met who was actually living it.

Her comment really touched me, and I wondered, am I really living that?

As I thought about it, I realized that I really was. I earn a living doing something I love. I travel to wonderful places and lead retreats, workshops, and courses full of amazing people, and I keep learning and growing all the time.

Over time, your dedication to what you love will transform your life in ways that allow you to spend more and more of your time doing what you are most passionate about.

It's inevitable, but you have to remember that this book isn't about creating the life of your dreams - it's about discovering how the life you're living right now is already the life of your dreams.

Ever since I first started living my passion, my life has felt entirely full, even during years when I was strapped with debt and had to work hard doing things that I didn't really love just to support myself.

The reason my life felt totally full was because I was more focused on the time I spent doing what I loved, than on what I had to do to support it. I was already living the life of my dreams.

And here's the point. You can always look at your problems and the challenges you face. There's always going to be things that aren't working, and time you must spend doing things you might not want to.

None of that makes your life any less abundant, because life is always full as long as you pay attention to the fullness. Realizing the fullness of life is what true abundance is.

My story is a good example of the shift into abundance because I didn't start out this way. Like most people, I was insecure and afraid a great deal of the time. It wasn't until I devoted my life to spiritual pursuit, the thing I was most passionate about, that things started changing dramatically for me.

At that point, I didn't care about being abundant. All I wanted to do was to meditate and explore spiritual ideas. I didn't care about money or possessions. I didn't worry about all the work it took to support myself. I felt totally full working hard and having very little because I was pursuing my passion with all my heart. I was abundant in the life I was living. I was living the life of my dreams, and over time, the abundance that I was living attracted even more abundance.

Realizing the fullness of life is what true abundance is.

DO WHAT YOU LOVE
BECAUSE YOU LOVE IT

The fifth principle of spiritual abundance is to forget about spiritual abundance and literally just do what you love.

I believe that the reason my life has been so full and abundant is because I was so totally devoted to pursuing what I loved the most. I wasn't doing it for any other reason than because I loved it. It wasn't a means to some other end for me; it was what I loved. And it still is what I love and what my life is all about. I am still living my passion.

I remember a book called *Do What You Love and the Money Will Follow*. To be honest, I've never read the book, but I now realize there was something that I would have added to the cover. You see in my opinion, that beautiful book title should have a subtitle that reads: *But Only If You're Not Doing It for the Money*. Because, if you're doing it for the money, you're not really doing what you love. You're using what you love to make money, and there's a big difference.

The first principle of abundance isn't: use your passion to get what you want. The first principle is: live your passion. Don't delay. Don't wait. If you live your passion throughout your entire life, how can that not possibly work out for the best? When you're living your passion, your entire life starts to align with what you're passionate about. And isn't that what we want? Isn't spiritual abundance about living a life that is centered on what we're truly passionate about?

My own life has included years of struggle, including many episodes of mounting debt. I'd get out of debt and go into more debt because, every time I made money, I used it to pursue more of what I was passionate about. And I didn't really care that I was in debt because I was doing what I loved. In a mysterious way, there was a momentum building during that time that now carries my life abundantly forward.

For any of you that are at a point where you're feeling the challenge and the struggle, I want you to know that I know there are times when the whole thing feels like a rock you have to push uphill. And the problem with pushing a rock uphill is that, if you're not actively pushing it up, then it's rolling back down on you. Pushing uphill requires constant effort. But, if you're doing what you love, it won't feel like effort because you're doing what you love.

And then, at some point, you start feeling the rock level off. You're not going uphill anymore. It's easier to push. So now you can rest a little if you want. And then you realize that your life is starting to move without your needing to push at all. It starts to move out of your hands. Your abundance and your success are happening on their own and you're almost having to run to catch up.

That is what happens in a life of abundance, but of course you were already doing what you loved so your life was already full anyway.

Once you realize that true abundance is possible right now, you won't want anyone to live any other way.

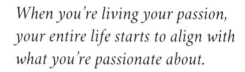
When you're living your passion, your entire life starts to align with what you're passionate about.

ABOUT THE AUTHOR

Jeff Carreira is a meditation teacher, mystical philosopher and author who teaches to a growing number of people throughout the world. As a teacher, Jeff offers retreats and courses guiding individuals in a form of meditation he refers to as The Art of Conscious Contentment. Through this simple and effective meditation technique, Jeff has led thousands of people in the journey beyond the confines of fear and self-concern into the expansive liberated awareness that is our true home.

Ultimately, Jeff is interested in defining a new way of being in the world that will move us from our current paradigm of separation and isolation into an emerging paradigm of unity and wholeness. He is exploring some of the most revolutionary ideas and systems of thought in the domains of spirituality, consciousness, and human development. He teaches people how to question their own experience so deeply that previously held assumptions about the nature of reality fall away to create space for dramatic shifts in understanding.

Jeff is passionate about philosophy because he is passionate about the power of ideas to shape how we perceive reality and how we live together. His enthusiasm for learning is infectious, and he enjoys addressing student groups and inspiring them to develop their own powers of inquiry. He has taught students at colleges and universities throughout the world.

Jeff is the author of numerous books including: *The Art of Conscious Contentment, No Place But Home, The Miracle of Meditation, The Practice of No Problem, Embrace All That You Are, Philosophy Is Not a Luxury, Radical Inclusivity, The Soul of a New Self,* and *Paradigm Shifting.*

For more about Jeff or to book him for a speaking engagement, visit: www.jeffcarreira.com

Made in the USA
Columbia, SC
24 March 2020